Press Play

Relationship Games for Forever Couples

Sarah Maxwell

Press Play

By Sarah Maxwell

All rights reserved. No part of this book may be reproduced or transmitted in any form or by any means, electronic or mechanical, including photocopying, recording or by any information storage and retrieval system, without written permission from the authors, except for the inclusion of brief quotations in a review. The Australian Copyright Act 1968 (the act) allows a maximum of one chapter or 10 per cent of the book, whichever is the greater, to be photocopied by any educational institution for its educational purposes provided that the educational institution (or body that administers it) has given a remuneration notice to the Copyright Agency Limited (CAL).

Quotes are attributed within the journal

Copyright © 2023 Sarah Maxwell

National Library of Australia Cataloguing-in-Publication entry

Author: Maxwell, Sarah

Title: Press Play

ISBN: 978-0-646-87450-0

A catalogue record for this book is available from the National Library of Australia

Contents

Introduction	5
Game 1: The State Shifter Game	9
Game 2: New Couple Script	19
Game 3: The Workout Swap	29
Game 4: Hubby Hobby meets Wifey Whim	39
Game 5: Creating your Paper Palace	51
Game 6: Date-Free	65
Game 7: Vision Boarding Your Common Dreams	77
Game 8: Vows Brought to Life	89
Game 9: Intimate-o-Meter	99
Game 10: Listen Up	109
Game 11: Couple ZZZs	121
Game 12: Get Jiggy with It	131

This book is dedicated to all couples striving to remain connected, loving and in appreciation of one another...

On average, relationships last seven to eight years – so, to all of you navigating well above the average, I salute you and your desire to continue to add value to your togetherness.

And so, my heartfelt gratitude goes out to my brave-heart Mother who had the courage to leave her "less-than-healthy" relationships so that I might strive for one that is healthy, strong and inspiring!

And to my forever-life-partner Nat, who always helps me find the light, funnier side of life, you *give me perspective, joy, and unconditional love!*

Introduction

I had a dream…

Ever since I was a little girl, I wanted to be in a forever, loving, and grounded relationship. I was deeply curious about "unconditional love" and seemed to be on high alert wherever I went for what it might look and feel like. Nothing could talk me out of my utopic view of a loving, committed relationship. Not my Mom's struggles with divorce, nor living the average North American upbringing of "blended family moving around to visit other parent" of which most of my friends were doing the same.

I still wanted it. I was sifting and sorting through life for that unconditionally loving partnership.

I could go on to explain all my heart-broken moments of love (as that's just part of the deal when you put yourself fully out there) but it's my current love affair of 23 years that I choose to share here. It is what inspired this book. The Games created in this book are what we still practice all these years later.

We met as professional athletes. I had only dated men, she, only women. We came together as friends. We started our relationship on less than solid ground. Coming from opposite places on the globe, it was combining my snowy northern self with her tropical heated self. And then, add the testing element that we competed against each other for our Olympic dream…

And yet, here we are, 23 years on with a 7-year-old Princess and a loving, creative relationship surrounded by our extended families. We married in New Zealand in 2008 (a union that felt solid and real to us and all our community that flew in) and again in 2018 on the heels of Australia legalizing Gay Marriage. There was such power in marrying again 10 years down the track. It became an opportunity to reflect on what we had lived together and vision our way forward toward our golden years.

Besides the laughter and humor that roams around our relationship, one of the key tenets we have always gone back to is our own relational development: mostly in the form of personal growth. I have found that every single time one of us engages in any form of development work, our relationship expands.

I'm not sure whether it was our sporting background or not, but we love to play GAMES. It can be board games or sporting matches; we just love how an activity can bring out the most innate parts of ourselves without the barrier of "looking good" thwarting the outcome.

I've always loved the quote, "As you Play, You Are". This is what inspired my background in BioPsychology to use Gamification as its vehicle. I would always ask myself: "How can I reflect this teaching in a fun, game-like format where people can bring their full selves to the experience without being distracted by how they "think" they should be behaving?" This leading question resulted in hundreds of 'Forever Couples' walking into my office and being introduced to light and fun communication games that stimulate connection.

My life passion is relationships. It's personal and professional. My own drive and motivation for courses and games I create are often stimulated by what I am trying to figure out in my own life and coupling. My lucky partner Nat has had to endure many a "pillow coaching" session (which we lovingly coined when I slip into "coach-mode" rather than remembering intimate relationships are NOT built like that!) I am sure she wishes the session would end an hour before it does. She has been known to say, "you keep talking, and I'll just sleep"! And yes, I do my best to not get mad that she dared say such a thing. I think you are beginning to see why humor is so vital for long-lasting relationships.

This book is the result of a spark of inspiration. I felt sure that these "aha moments" my personal clients were having should be available to all "forever couples". It's not for some, it's for all. We all can grow and expand our love, connection and appreciation for one another.

Now, it's your turn to...

Go forth and Press Play on your relationship!

Sarah Maxwell

Brisbane, Australia

February 2023

Game 1

The State Shifter Game

On Your Marks: From Moody to Masterful

Do you or your partner ever get moody? Is "I'm not a morning person" or "I just need time to unwind after work" something you hear regularly?

Emotional stamina is generally not something we work on unless we must, so it is no wonder that moodiness is considered an acceptable excuse in relationships in Western society. If our emotions are a choice, why does it sometimes feel like our reaction was the only possibility at that moment?

"To cease smoking is the easiest thing I ever did. I ought to know; I've done it 1,000 times," Mark Twain reportedly said.

Changing habits is thought to be one of the toughest things to do because, on some level, we know we should just snap out of it. We tell ourselves to 'stop it' and move on. But, after much frustration and feeling disappointment in ourselves, we abandon all hope of changing and claim, "this is just who I am." But is it?

Imagine being able to shift state with the snap of your fingers and living a reality where you are in charge of your mood, with the ability to flex around in varying emotional states at will. What could this mean for your intimate relationship? If you and your partner chose your moods and could move out of negative spaces in an instant, how would that shift your experience of life?

It really can be that easy. Once the foundation is laid with this State Shifter Game, you can enact it daily, with the true value felt months later when you're living a relationship free of emotional build-up and stagnation.

Get Set: Re-Defining Change

Former British Prime Minister Harold Wilson cut to the chase when he said, "He who rejects change is the architect of decay. The only human institution which rejects progress is the cemetery." The definition of change involves words like transform, alter, conform, substitute, become different, and modify. Each of these words contains the essence of movement. It's shifting away from what something would have been if left alone. Think about deconstructing the meaning of change even further, as the words we use can slip past our comprehension and lose the power they initially contained. What if changing or shifting was a decision point within each moment to either:

Choose a better feeling thought or

Choose a worse feeling thought.

There would be no in-between or neutral stances, just directionality and movement.

In basketball, a key footwork technique that helps the player change direction is called 'the pivot'. A player's weight might be entirely on one foot and then transferred to the other to change tack and be able to shift position on point. These decision points or pivot opportunities are there in life whether we acknowledge them consciously or not. The source of the pivot in this basketball example is the player, and it would be beneficial to look at the source of change rather than the movement itself. If change is inevitable, then our relationship to it seems like an interesting component.

Real empowerment is when we are deliberate about change, and the direction we choose to head in. It is fun and exciting when we are active participants in the process of change. As is the game I am presenting here.

"Change always comes bearing gifts," says Chairman and CEO Price Pritchett. So, the opportunity for blessings is yours as you play this revolutionary State Shifter Game.

Go: How to Play

You will require two players who agree to play full out (no matter how goofy or silly you feel - the more playful you are, the more laughs you'll get out of this.)

Choose the person who will go first. They must decide on a nursery rhyme they can recount for three minutes. The other person's role will be to time the three minutes and call out "shift" every 30 seconds or so.

It is imperative in the recounting of the nursery rhyme to employ full-body actions and differing voices/tonality to make it as compelling as possible. This is a physiological tool and vital to the process.

Whenever you hear the word "SHIFT", you must immediately change tack and alter the story dramatically.

For example: If Little Red Riding Hood is leisurely walking down the wooded path and you hear "shift", she may then be running and screaming crazily through the woods while singing a rock song.

Once the three minutes have passed with six or so "shifts" called, reverse the roles and have the other person choose a different nursery rhyme and repeat the process.

Going the Distance: Taking it to the Real Game of Life

Now that you have both played this fun little game, here are some key questions to write down and pen some answers to:

What I learned in this exercise was?

Where in my life do I resist change?

What have I done in the past when the need to change has presented itself?

When I saw myself able to change and be creative, I felt…

The power of this game is in its future implementation. You and your partner can agree to call "shift" in everyday life situations. If both engage in the process, you choose to shift states on the spot and radically change the direction of your relationship. It's only in the playing that you will discover this for yourself.

Eternal lovers
Taino Central America symbols

The symbol of the eternal lovers is usually shown as birds connected by their beaks, or a possible love scene. For the Taino, eternal love was important. As there was no belief in private property, everything that was grown or killed belonged to the entire tribe.

The eternal lovers represent equality amongst the tribe as well as fertility.

Meet The Players:

Wendy and Walter

Montreal, Canada

Adapted from an interview with 10-year-strong couple Wendy & Walter from Montreal, Canada.

Wendy was first introduced to The State Shifter Game through an individual coaching session, and this was her reaction to it.

"When I was first introduced to the game, it sounded great, and I was willing to play. I presented it to Walter, and he was willing to play too. Games are fun, and it didn't seem like homework or work, and it was easy to play. It's childlike, you just jump in and there's no pressure at all. I was most surprised at how easy it was to change my mood on the spot, as I didn't think I would be able to do that. After we'd tried it, I did wonder how it would go in real life when I was really pissed off."

For Walter, it wasn't as easy initially. "At first, it was hard. Wendy told me to change my mood, and I was thinking I didn't feel like changing my mood. But then I remembered it was part of the process, so I thought, ok, I'll give it a try. In the beginning, it was hard, but it got easier. Then it was my turn to tell her to shift and I thought that was totally fun. When she wasn't in the best of moods or when it was time for her mood to change, I would shout 'SHIFT'. Shifting and changing is good, you know. I could see there were times she didn't want to shift, but because we set out the rules or because that's the game, then you must change. I am stubborn. I think it's more that I don't want to change when someone else is telling me to do it. If I want to change, I'll change myself or do it when I want to, but when someone is telling me to change right then on the spot, I feel the 'no' rising. I've realised it before, but I think the game brought it out more."

But was it worth it for Walter? "Yep, because I see the results and it totally changes the mood. Whether we've had an argument or been screaming about something, once one of us changed, you can see the immediate effect for the better."

Wendy reflected on what she has seen change since playing this game. "We don't have those wasted evenings of one of us being pissed off and kind of writing the night off because it ends right there when someone calls "shift". And so, there's less bad time and more quality time, happy time, relaxation time, whatever it is. So that's been the biggest impact, less crappy time together and lots more great times!"

When asked what playing a simple three-minute game was worth to her, Wendy said: "time is worth everything. We can never get time back, right? In the past, when I had a wasteful night because I was remaining in my pissy mood, I'd be so angry about it. I'd be like, 'ugh, here's what could have been a potential awesome evening with my husband, and it's gone' like it's been wasted. And so, it is worth everything. Those are moments you can't get back and why waste them trying to uphold some silly principle that doesn't even really matter?"

Game 2

New Couple Script

On Your Marks: The Joy of Being the Director

We are constantly living out the story of our lives. But rare is the one who is conscious about it. Only in retrospect do we make commentary, resolve to do better, or merely justify our actions by shifting blame onto others. If you had the choice between deliberately creating your life story (akin to being the scriptwriter and director of your life's blockbuster movie) or merely reacting to it as it unfolds, which would you choose? We are all creating whether we know it consciously or not, so being deliberate about it opens an opportunity for absolute joy and fulfilment.

Imagine how empowering it is for movie director Steven Spielberg as he imagines and creates leading-edge scripts such as ET and brings them to life on the big screen for children and adults to enjoy. Writing a script is a powerful experience that is confirmed when life's events match up with it. Writing the story of your life is how you take control of your destiny and infuse it with all the saucy, fun, enriching experiences you desire.

Focusing specifically on your intimate relationship and scripting it with flair, fun and poise is nothing short of magical. Every part of your life warrants scripting, but to focus on a particular subject, such as love and relationship, is so rewarding. Once you begin the process and relax into it, you will understand how juicy this really is. It's no accident that we are birthed with imagination, even if many of us have experienced its erosion since that time, so give yourself permission to be the Spielberg of your own life.

After personally living the fruits of such story writing as an athlete and then in my intimate relationship, my answer to why write a new couple story is thunderously "why the heck not?"

Get Set: Living at the Forefront of your Life

Truth merely equals beliefs that large masses of people share and then recycle over and over again. And if a belief is simply a thought we keep thinking, then this sacrosanct thing we call reality can only be a compounded thought repeated so often it appears as a factual matter. In The Power of Awareness, Neville Goddard summed it up by stating, "Your mind is always arranged in the image of all you believe and consent to as true."

What if we could decide what thoughts we produce at source? If all reality stems from these originating thoughts, it's about time to get in front of this whole thing and create what we truly want. Imagine living out your life rather than watching it as an after-effect. By taking a different stance on your life, you can literally design desired outcomes from known events. All it takes is a shift in where you view your life from. It's time to stand out in front and be in the desire fulfilled. No longer shall it feel like a wish list (which brings up the feelings of 'not having') but rather a 'have done' list, which feels so refreshing.

The transcendental expert of our time, Dr Wayne Dyer, has coined three distinct levels how we evolve through of life:
1) After a life event occurs, one reflects after the fact on what could have been done differently to learn from it.
2) In the midst of an event, we consciously make a shift in the moment based on what we are experiencing.
3) Living at the forefront of one's life by scripting with deliberate intention.

Dr Dyer recommends we move through these levels of evolution throughout our lifetime, but ultimately, living out in front of one's life is the way of the sage.

Go: How to Write Your Script

Each member of the couple will be journaling. Commit to writing at least one paragraph. The theme of this process is to write a new story for your relationship from your vantage point five years down the track. Place that date five years in the future at the top of your page and be as free flowing as if it were a fairy tale. However, this is your life, your desires, and your outcomes. It's your private script, and no one else will see it unless you show it to them. Feel the freedom of being the boss of your own story.

From that standpoint, reflect on all the fantastic things that have transpired over the past years using words such as have, did, completed, enjoyed, loved, experienced, and relaxed. "In order to make a future wish a present fact, you must assume the feeling of the wish fulfilled," coined Goddard. Step fully into the picture so you can feel, see, hear, and taste it. Once you get in the flow, it will seem like it's writing itself. If you find yourself diverging into other areas of your life, go with it. Your relationship touches every part of your life, so this is likely to occur.

Be gentle with yourself as you may find yourself thinking thoughts like 'this isn't real' or 'I have to be honest with myself'. This is perfectly natural. We are often very committed to scripts that have been playing out for a lifetime, so when something new is introduced, you may encounter resistance. Champion yourself along, knowing it takes stamina to direct and orchestrate the show. If you find yourself writing effortlessly, enjoy the experience. Remember to add as much detail as you can afford yourself.

Three pages are suggested as long enough and short enough to get the desired experience. It's something to aim for and nothing more scientific than that. Enjoy your director's chair!

Going the Distance: Buried Dreams Come to Life

The vital component for this process to work long after you've written your script is this - fold your script and put it somewhere sacred where it won't be revealed for at least five years. That's a big call.

This real-life story should inspire you to the power of adopting the sacred elements contained in the New Couple Script. Introducing the woman known for 'burying her dreams': Tererai Trent of Zimbabwe. Tererai is an awe-inspiring woman who developed a list of goals for herself as a young girl living in a rural village. Her list was buried in a piece of tin behind her home in a field where she herded cattle. Unable to go to school as a child because of being born female, she secretly did her brother's homework until her father found out and married her off at age 11. Having three children by age 18 with an abusive husband, she quickly divorced him the moment the family landed in America. Over the next 20 years, she accomplished every goal in her tin can - earning a bachelor's and master's degrees from Western Michigan University and completing her journey from life as an impoverished African child bride to a career as an international scholar who holds a PhD. Each time she returned to Zimbabwe, she dug up the list, crossed off the achieved goal and moved on to the next one.

I am not asking you to bury your journal in the backyard, but I am suggesting your life can be as prolific and inspiring as that of Tererai Trent. There is no need to revisit your script continually. The work was complete when you wrote the story. That is all it takes to align your desires. When you put your script away, you are unconsciously allowing your blessed life to come to pass.

Triskeles
Celtic Love Knot

The Triskeles, sometimes known as a "Celtic love knot", is one of the oldest Celtic symbols. The three sides represent earth, water and fire. The continuous line represents love, unity and eternal life. The significance of the three sides is unknown, though some symbologists suggest a connotation of motion, movement or energy.

Meet the Players:

Allan and Lari

Sydney, Australia

Adapted from the interview with Australian couple Lari & Allan, who have been together 24 years (on the eve of their family embarking on yet another life adventure: moving interstate)

Meeting at university, Lari and Allan's relationship blossomed and moved them to Japan, where they both found self-development in grieving for their firstborn dying in their expectant arms. They have been open to expanding who they are in the world since then.

This might explain why Allan found this experience "easy...just writing and flowing with it."

He did say, "I'm very analytical at times and I just kept thinking about it. And given the ages (of his daughters) made it easier."

Analytical or not, Allan knows that "It's all about getting clear on your vision and moving towards your own truth. Because when I was doing the scripting in this game, I was reminding myself to remain in my heart space and speak to myself from there. That ensured that everything I wrote focused on what was true to me."

Lari approached it by getting herself centered and to "...just be in a meditative childlike state of wonder where everything's possible. And then, right from that space, I put the date in the corner, in five years - 2027. I wrote to Allan and just talked about all the things that had unfolded over the past five years (in past tense), plus what I was excited for in the future as well."

Lari proceeded to share their daily practice (listen to the live podcast interview at www.buzzsprout.com/238055/11755643) while Allan highlighted that "…every big decision we make, we ask the key question: Is it true to us?"

One of my favorite things Lari said during this conversation was, "We don't want to have a crisis just to propel ourselves forward."

This is a great reminder to us all to use a daily structure that works for our coupling well before the 'relationship vultures' start circling. Write your script with wonder and joy and remain centered in the heart like Allan and Lari. And then, relish in the adventure that life has in store for you.

Game 3

The Workout Swap

On Your Marks: Slip into Their Nike's

It's not often you get to squeeze into someone else's Nike Frees. This is your chance to dive your feet in (metaphorically speaking), tie the laces and experience what your partner feels when getting fit and healthy.

Creating a workout for your mate is a multi-faceted activity. On the one hand, you're imagining your partner doing exercises and how you want the experience to be for them as well as performing the workout proposed to you. You get diversification of your regular routine and to experience, for a moment, what it might be like to be in your partner's shoes. Seeing life from another's vantage point is interesting, adventuresome and refreshing. It's experiencing the world through a new, fresh perspective.

Let's be clear here; this is not about making your partner suffer the way you do so they can sympathise with your daily pain. Instead, it's an opportunity to show your mate how you spend your 'sweating' hours either in the gym, running on the road or downward dogging it up.

A bi-product of creating workouts for one another is variety in your training. Rather than struggling to come up with new and exciting ways to move your body, jump into the designed workout from your partner and provide a fresh, new workout for your mate too. What a nice alternative to an expensive personal trainer, the free version lying next to you each night.

Get Set: Variety as the Spice of Life?

They say that variety is the spice of life, but what does that even mean? Do we really need spice to live? Father of Self-Development, Anthony Robbins, would say "yes" to that as he has coined 'Variety' as one of the six basic needs of the human spirit along with certainty, significance, love/connection, growth and contribution.

Often, our need for certainty rubs up against our need for variety, so one way that both needs are met is to have a routine. For example, working out three days a week in the mornings but varying the workout so one morning it's Pilates, the next might be a run, and the third morning you go to the gym. Robbins claims that if we do not get our needs met in healthy ways, they will fill themselves in any way possible, even if that is negative. I liken it to a pair of jeans that are too tight; no matter how hard we push down the fat, those rolls somehow find their way to the surface and spill over the waistband. By this definition, it would be in our best interest to be proactive about the variety we insert into our lives. Leaving it up to chance might have even more dramatic consequences than a muffin top.

Started in 1995, CrossFit as a fitness regimen has taken the world by storm. Taking the athletes' mindset for training and layering it onto fitness into consideration, the main philosophy for getting striking results is, "Our prescription or methodology for achieving this elite fitness is constantly varied, if not randomised, functional movements executed at (relatively) high intensity," says CrossFit founder Greg Glassman. In fitness, variety breeds great results without much time required. The formula is clear, so why not get on board? Your partner providing variety in your life through a fun activity is ticking many boxes.

Go: Designing the Workout

If you want to put maximum effort into this, before drafting up your official workout, fill out the following checklist as a guide to designing something worth presenting to your loved one.

Partner A's Design	
Intention of Workout	
Duration	
Partner's Strengths	
Partner's Weaknesses	
Exercises	
Goal/benchmark for them to reach	
Why you chose these exercises?	

Now that you have some direction, draft a written workout in point form and present it to you partner.

Allow them to read and take it all in and then here comes the fun part...teach them how to do the exercises and inspire them to complete your workout.

The more thoughtful you are about this process, the more you will get out of it.

It's not just about the design, it's about how you present it and 'sell' it to your mate.

Bring forth the personal trainer within.

Going the Distance: Fit for Love

So, how far can you take this? Well, a couple in Melbourne, Australia, has run over 60 marathons, crossing the finish line hand-in-hand. Now that's together-ness! What started as a one-off race where wife Sue suggested, "I will run with you for a bit, but I can't go that far," and Andrew replying, "I reckon we should just stick together," has turned into a movement called Partner Running. Running 50km each week for ten years and completing marathons from Chicago to South Africa, they have written a book called Couple on the Run with their motto being, "It was this amazing thing that we crossed the finish line together. Running together changed our whole relationship ... we've got no phones, no TV; we end up talking and communicating."

(Excerpts from Andrew and Sue O'Brien Couple on the Run)

(Excerpts from the Sydney Morning Herald) http://www.smh.com.au/sport/secret-of-longdistance-feats-down-to-crossing-the-line-hand-in-hand-20100919-15i06.html#ixzz1WUjYuWfq)

Though we may not have a desire to run around the globe with our partner, exercising with one another can truly shift your relationship to a new dimension. Any shared experience becomes a connection point, but getting fit and healthy along with that, is a recipe for longevity. American car giant Henry Ford coined the phrase, "Coming together is a beginning. Keeping together is progress. Working together is success." It's one thing to practice this activity once but incorporating it as part of your daily routine, is real success.

Mixing it up and designing workouts for one another releases endorphins, shifts mental state, and leads to longevity of life and exuberant vitality. The formula is so simple that it's only a matter of starting. Get sweaty together and reap the benefits.

Meet the Players:

Leah and Todd

Vancouver, Canada

Beautiful Vancouver, British Columbia couple Leah & Todd had been dating for 11 months when this interview took place on August 29th, 2011.

(More than ten years on, they have two children, have done their master's and have recently moved cities)

Leah and Todd created a brilliant activity. Leah claims it was a joint decision that mostly came from her teasing Todd about how boring triathlons would be, but Todd was eager to spend some active time together.

When prodded as to the idea behind designing workouts for one another, Leah thoughtfully commented, "It creates an appreciation for both the activity, the person is in and the amount of work they put into it. It also changed the dynamics of our relationship and conversation because in having Todd teach and coach me, we experienced each other in a new and exciting way."

Although Todd was much more matter of fact about it and into the logistics of creating a sound training session, he did reflect that, "She's much more accomplished as an athlete than I am, and she commented a lot about how different and difficult the training is in triathlon. Although I don't think she understands my motivation, it's nice to feel some appreciation for it, especially from someone so good in her sport." You can detect from Todd that it feels nice to be appreciated and understood.

The creating process was different for both, as Todd was in charge. His thoughts on it were, 'The creation was a no-brainer because I do triathlons all the time. The only thought that had to go into it was to plan the time and distances of all three sports so Leah would get a decent workout in without it being a bad experience." Notice the consideration here for his mate. Leah commented that she was grateful that Todd tailored the workout to some of her strengths as well so that all the experience was rewarding.

The benefits have reached far beyond that one workout, as sensed when Leah says, "Working out is such a huge part of each of our lives that we can now share together. For both of us, the time is special, and even when we don't talk at all during our workouts, we feel really connected."

Todd carries that even further with his deep belief that, "There's an element of intention required. Activities rarely happen without some planning involved. There's a goal, steps to get there, teamwork involved in achieving it, measurable progress, and the fruits of the effort. I really believe that the technique involved in setting those things up will spill over to other areas in our relationship. We get to develop a way of getting things done and can often apply it to other things, as small as getting to a family dinner together or as big as building a future we both dream of."

Game 4

Hubby Hobby meets Wifey Whim

On Your Marks: Mirror, Mirror on the Wall

What do you get when you respect, honour and appreciate another? The obvious answer might be about being of service to someone else and putting them ahead of yourself and how that feels good. But I want to suggest a gain even grander than that...a connection with the core of your Inner Being.

Basically, the way we view others is the way we view ourselves and so to appreciate another is to essentially honour ourselves. Our partner is a mere reflection of us, which explains why so many marriages end in divorce. The hardest thing can be to look ourselves in the mirror, especially when we judge what we see.

Do you know any couples who nag, judge, or seem annoyed with each other? Do you know them intimately? We all go there sometimes and so be gentle with yourself if this is you. Someone occurring annoying is said to be a part of ourselves that we don't accept. Pretty full-on words if you find yourself holding some strong opinions of others.

Now, imagine allowing, respecting, and loving your partner and this becoming the new you. Relationships (relating-ships) at their core, symbolise a bouncing-off place for us to grow and expand. It facilitates the more challenging life learnings such as self-acceptance and self-love because we can allow ourselves to do it more easily for another.

Rather than trying to clean up your act through self-punishment or denial, take a moment to think about what your partner most loves to do (and which you have been unwilling to participate in in the past) and then plot your 'Hubby Hobby meets Wifey Whim' experience. Gains are experiences two-fold: on the giving end because you're giving a gift to your partner as well as yourself, but also on the receiving end because you're sharing your favourite activity with the one you love.

Get Set: Acceptance Kicks Tolerance's Butt!

After interviewing couples who have been married for over 30 years, the common thread of their love and longevity together was respect and honouring their partner as they are and not trying to change them into what they believed they should be.

A common misconception when hearing this would be to tolerate your loved one to survive through the challenges of time. There is a clear line being drawn between acceptance and tolerance. Acceptance is not heavy, burdensome, nor an 'I have to' but rather an allowing of the other to be free to be completely themselves.

Former US President Barrack Obama and his wife Michelle commented the following when asked what they tell young people about marriage today, "It has to be a true partnership. You really must like and respect the person you're married to because it's a hard road. Don't expect it to be easy. Melding two lives and trying to raise others and doing it forever, that's a recipe for disaster. So, there are highs and lows, but if in the end, you can look him in the eye and say, I like you". Michelle further commented, "The wonderful love stage fades, and you need a little bit more."

And that little bit more is practicing the art of allowing, accepting, and honouring your bedmate day in and day out. Being deliberate and overt can be the best recipe for success because months melt into years and decades before you recognise you haven't ever watched a football match with your husband, and he has never been to the ballet.

Don't fall off your chair thinking about the dread of either of those activities but rather frame it as your opportunity to experience something new, something through the eyes of your companion for life.

Go: Choosing, Planning and Executing the Grand Activity

List your partner's top three favourite activities/hobbies (without showing nor discussing them with your partner)

1.

2.

3.

Once you have narrowed the list down, it is vital you have not participated in the activity with your mate in the past; or that it's been more than five years since you have. The choice you make for your activity should be based on what they would most enjoy, not what you can most likely tolerate. Your ears won't pop at the Opera boys, nor gals will your nail polish chip off when the fishing line brings up your first catch on that remote fishing trip.

Activities can range in timing and scale. It may involve taking a plane or simply reading books in bed one night. There are no comparing activities based on scale, price, longevity, or complexity. Own what you choose for the other and relish the activity selected for you as its sacred ground when someone considers you wholeheartedly.

This next phase presents some options. After you organise your activity, you can either tell your partner about it, if them getting excited is something that adds to the exercise, or you can keep your cards close to your chest and make it a grand surprise on the day. It's important to consider whether it's you that likes surprises or them because this is about imagining what they would be most pleased with.

Another element that heightens this experience is to avoid being covertly convinced to discuss your option choices with your mate. They may want to get their claws into your choice of activity and tell you what they love most...breathe and keep your cards breasted as this allows the exercise to be that much richer. Even control freaks can use a bit of rest and relaxation.

Going the Distance: We are What we Repeatedly Do.

Bringing this exercise into your everyday life will make all the difference. Doing anything once is an insight but building a habit of 'being', defines a life. Aristotle seconds that by saying, "We are what we repeatedly do. Excellence, then, is not an act but a habit." Begin thinking of your relationship in terms of excellence. We have been surviving them for too long; it's now the era of thriving.

Obviously, if you begin to get in the groove of thinking about what your partner enjoys doing and then stepping outside of your comfort zone to do that, your relationship can only grow deeper. Taking this exercise and making it a habit is what brings power to the process. Experiences teach, so repeating them can only augment your happiness and fulfilment quotient.

We often hesitate to extend ourselves too much or too often in case our partner gets too used to it. Believe it or not, it has the opposite effect. It encourages your partner to come your way and want to explore your world more regularly. But you can't do it for that reason. Being genuine and pure in your endeavour is everything.

This process gets easier. The introduction of 'Hubby Hobby meets Wifey Whim' can be likened to the tremendous effort required to get a turbine moving. Once it gains momentum, it moves itself with only occasional prompting required.

Now that your mind has been tuned to this idea, it will come up with new ways to excite your partner with fluidity and rhythm. Activities may be smaller but no less impactful. Your relationship will become defined by thoughtfulness, appreciation and deep respect.

You will be the inspiration of all your friends, and when they come asking, "How come your relationship is so good?" you can be sure to describe that quirky exercise you did way back when and how it all started with Hubby's Hobby and a Wifeys Whim.

Meet the Players:

Jane and Michael

Perth, Australia

Jane & Mike hail from Perth, Australia and are some of the original digital nomads travelling the world house-sitting. Authors of over 90 books, they explore the beauty of life through photography and mapping the furthest reaches of the vast landscape of Australia.

(This excerpt of this interview was recorded in 2011).

This game required thoughtful planning and an adventurous spirit and so this was the ideal couple to bring that to life. Mike asked Jane to marry him during a 12-day hike in outback Western Australia, proving they are attuned to adventure with a bit of planning.

Mike got straight into it by considering what Jane was into, even though it wasn't his cup of tea normally. "She's musical," he thought, "so why not the Opera!" He commented, "This is something I'd never do in a million years. I really had no interest in going, but I thought that would be something a little bit different. And surprise, surprise, I enjoyed it!" But it did take something for Mike to ensure that it was an activity totally for Jane and not one he tended towards.

Jane had to warm into it as her first ideas were things she was also into and so she stretched herself further and noticed the perfect thing. "I saw ads for fishing. Mike has always wanted to learn fly fishing, so I booked lessons for us both. It was amazing and a really interesting experience."

It seems magical that both partners loved their experiences, but Jane was quick to notice pieces of herself emerging when she remarked, "I knew Mike had organised something for me, and I wanted to jump in and control it. I don't like surprises particularly, so I was keen to know what he was doing, and how he was organising it. That was probably my biggest learning. I definitely like to control everything." But through this, she agreed, "It was fantastic to see that Mike can organise without me pushing him along and I can just let go."

Jane reminds us that you need to have a level of trust in the process when playing this one, "The timing was a bit short in terms of bookings, so up until the last minute, I didn't know whether it was going to come off or not. But it did!"

Well done you two. Still learning and growing after 30 years of marriage.

Game 5

Creating Your Paper Paradise

On Your Marks: Reality Catching up with your Imaginings

Building your dream home is one of the fairy tale goals of couples in Western society. Knowing this to be true, it was quite surprising for me to introduce 'Building Your Paper Paradise' to my private couple clients and observe them not even knowing what they wanted as individuals nor what their mate fancied either. After years of being together, how could a great couple not have an inkling of what could make up their mutual oasis?

It basically boils down to not prioritising this conversation on desire nor creating the necessary time to test out ideas. People get busy with their everyday lives and forget what they once dreamed of. A mere 15-minute opportunity of coming together as a unit and building your dream home with paper and sticky tape can catapult partnerships into their mortar and brick paradise.

What is the cost of having a dream go unfulfilled? A life half-lived is very painful and stories of death-bed regret are rampant. With a process and 'how to' at your fingertips, there are no more excuses for having something you imagined not be realised.

A concrete-built structure standing in front of your very eyes is so much more powerful than a mere discussion. It can start there, but this takes it one step further. This is a critical part of the recipe of realisation. "Words don't teach, you have to have your own personal experience in order to have that knowing," teaches Law of Attraction Guru Abraham.

If you want reality to catch up with your imaginings, then a tangible, concrete 3D structure is the way to go. When something takes shape before your very eyes, it aligns your cells and creates a neural connection that matches actual wooden floorboards, a roof over your head, and a pool with crystal clear water lapping in the backyard.

53

Get Set: Architect Modelling

What's the value in building a model of your dream before the actual construction takes place? For that answer, examining the methodology of one of the most respected visionaries of our time seemed appropriate. While on a business trip in the 1940s, Walt Disney drew sketches of his ideas for an amusement park where families could play in a safe and clean environment. Spending five years developing Disneyland, it was a team of 'Imagineers' who created aerial drawings of the park and used those three-dimensional prospects to bring to life a place visited by more than 600 million people since its opening in 1955.

Architects utilise models all the time as a means of facilitating communication on complicated or unusual designs, as it's a practical and open-ended method of exploring ideas. Designing and building rough models allows them to look at things from a different angle while opening-up dialogue between the many members of a project team.

Couples partnering to build something commonly loved, such as a dream home, would do well to adopt the same method. Weaving two lives into one beautiful home is no easy feat! Former American First Lady, Michelle Obama spoke it plainly when commenting, "Melding two lives and trying to raise others and doing it forever…that's a recipe for disaster." The happy intertwining of two lives is an art that not many relationships have mastered.

Creating your Paper Paradise is a proposed training ground that produces a workable model for your dreams. Wouldn't it be more economical to scrunch up a piece of A4 paper than tear down a concrete wall that just didn't work?

Couples often wait for the architect to arrive and the builders to commence their project before realising they are not clear on what they want. Here is your chance to get your hands in the proverbial clay of your relationship and mold your dream home.

Go: Your Dream Home Rising

The objective of the Creating your Paper Paradise exercise is to build your dream home in 15 minutes or less. The only building materials allotted are paper (white or coloured), sticky tape, and scissors. Armed with these materials, set a stopwatch for 15 minutes, and you must plan, construct and finalise your paper paradise in that time.

Make the exercise truly powerful by building in 3D. Of course, colour will only enhance the outcome. Testing your structure for durability and stability is to be done via the 'blow test.' Blow as hard as you can near your home's bottom, middle and top. Does it withstand this wind gust? Knowing that wind and weather can disrupt the integrity of your home, it's up to you to secure its foundations and fortify those elements requiring more stability.

(Hint: foundations are the crux of a home surviving the test of time. Give it its due attention.)

You can keep your structure somewhere visible as a reminder of your dream home or take a photo and place it where it can be seen often. Your final product not only symbolises your dream but also your capacity to work as a team to combine shared desires. This is no small feat and so display it with pride. Others will wonder what you've got there, and you can tell the story of your training. This only reinforces your actual dream home as well as inspiring others to create for themselves too. Win-Win.

Working as a team is paramount, and your communication skills will be tested as there is no time to dawdle. Recommendations are to quickly pour out ideas and then come up with a building plan. No idle hands or double-handling means both members of the couple being active in their individual roles while coming together when it's time to join pieces.

Going the Distance: Using symbolism to adopt new relational strategies

Once you have built your dream home, fill in the table exampled below with ten different structure elements (e.g. garage, kitchen, staircase, pool, backyard, walls, windows, roof, etc.)

STRUCTURE	DIRECT USE	SYMBOLISM (RELATIONSHIP)
Etc...		

Now, take each structural element and create symbolisms as they relate to your relationship using the following process:

STRUCTURE	DIRECT USE	SYMBOLISM (RELATIONSHIP)
GARAGE	A place to park cars and store bigger, unsightly items.	Parking work issues and dramas in a specific place reserved for them.
Etc…		

How can you use this symbolism to benefit your relationship? Using the example above, commit to parking your issues in the garage with the car and reserve your home for love, connection, and appreciation. This creates wonderful boundaries that promote nurture and growth inside the home.

As with all games, the power is in their daily implementation. If your 'Paper Paradise' becomes a symbol for new boundaries, places of joy within your relationship, shelter for your heart, freedom for your soul and colour of expression of emotion, those 15 minutes were worth their weight in gold.

The tangible building exercise re-aligns cells, but the actual consistent use of the symbology expands you and your relationship to a place never reached.

To infinity and beyond!

Padme Lotus
Ashtamangala Asia

The Padme, or Lotus, represents purity, illumination, love, growth and transformation. If the Lotus has eight petals, it symbolizes harmony, while a lotus with one thousand petals symbolizes enlightenment. A lotus seed or bud represents potential. "Om mane padme." is a Buddhist mantra, which translates as 'the jewel in the lotus'. It means that there is potential for enlightenment in each of us. The color of the Padme can also change its meaning. White symbolizes purity and spiritual perfection. Red, passion and love. A blue lotus bud signifies intelligence and communication. A pink flower represents transcendence.

Meet the Players:

Dimity and Josh

Brisbane, Australia

Young couple Dimity & Josh are recently engaged and now living in Brisbane, Australia in their newly purchased unit.

As these two vibrant 20-somethings start knitting their lives together, there is no better time to build a 'Paper Paradise' before the real thing comes knocking. They've bought their first unit together; they have launched a small business together, and now they are planning their wedding. It's all happening in their world.

So many interesting things arose as they played this game.

They are a busy, working couple and yet Dimity explains, "We played the game on a Friday night: we got some takeout and did it on our kitchen bench. I luckily have a craft storage in my apartment."

Josh acknowledges, "It was fun because Dimity is usually the artsy one, but this time I thought, I'll give it a go. I was trying to put those roles to the test and look at them. For me, this project was like a masterpiece in terms of what we're doing in our lives right now."

Dimity followed that up with, "Josh really led the architecture of the project while I was in more the dream state. I would dream up something and Josh would execute it. It was quite interesting to see how we both worked as a partnership. You could really see our personality traits coming out in how the project came together."

When they were finished with their 'Paper Paradise,' Josh exclaimed, "We're very clear on what we want as a couple," yet Dimity saw something even more clearly in the finale. "It made me realise that he needed his own space and wanted a man cave in his house. Allowing each other to have their own passions and space is so important. Because Josh has a lot of things he's passioned about, he does take up a lot of space. But maybe I didn't realise until we did this game how important and critical that is to Josh thriving in our relationship."

Seeing them both notice new and important pieces of each other during this game and then reflecting it back to one another made my heart soar. This is what these games are all about, learning and growing together. Seeing your mate in a different light and then being able to communicate acceptance and empathy for one another. Being such a young couple invested in their own development was very refreshing.

Game 6

Date-Free

On Your Marks: Distractions Be Gone

The standard fare of couples worldwide is the infamous 'date'. There is an entire movement based on it...online dating. Of the 54 million singles in the United States, 5.5 million use dating sites. That sure is a lot of dates going on in America! The question is: how many of those dates don't cost a dime? Date-Free is about using your creativity to design a date where no money changes hands, only pure-uninhibited relating-ship.

By eliminating the distractions that money can sometimes bring, the focus returns to the two members of the couple and quality time spent together. Simplicity is the name of the game. Returning to a time when technology did not occupy our every finger stroke and finding beauty in nature once more is the creed of this playful activity. There is a stillness and quiet that befalls the couple willing to step out of the norm and discover realms not often experienced within a typical date.

Not only are distractions sifted out so quality can rise to the surface, but you also save money. Date-Free is the gift that keeps on giving. When you take dollars off the table, you are suddenly thrown into a whole new way of thinking. Love, connection and appreciation come into focus and the shiny, sparkly things that initially attract become dull and faded.

Any time you change things up, you will be rewarded. Stepping out of the mundane routine of daily life as a couple reveals new components within your mate that fan the flames of romance and intimacy. When you remove those elements standing between you and your partner, you find yourself proximal to that sweet-smelling, loving creature you fell in love with. All that and at no extra charge.

Get Set: Free of Charge

Most couples understand the need for a date night after many years of being together. But brain and behaviour researchers insist that many couples may be going about it all wrong. "Couples need to tailor their date nights around new and different activities they both enjoy," says Arthur Aron, a professor of social psychology at the State University of New York at Stony Brook. "The goal is to find ways to keep injecting novelty into the relationship."

When engaging in a unique experience, the brain's reward system is activated and releases neurotransmitters dopamine and norepinephrine. This is the same circuitry which lit up when a couple was first enamoured and exhilarated by one another.

The creativity and novelty required to plan and experience a Date-Free night is right up your brain chemistry's alley. Now, mix that cocktail while eliminating one of relationships biggest buzz-killers, finances, and you have a match made in heaven. "Statistics still show that money is one of the leading causes of conflict and divorce," write Broussard and Burns, founders of the Romance and Finance Couple's Money Counseling Group. "When you create a forum where one of the biggest complaints is not even present, there is no choice but for a great experience."

A revolutionary book on relationships, The Five Love Languages by Gary Chapman, has one of its main languages as 'Quality Time.' Defining quality is key here as watching sports while sitting next to each other doesn't qualify as it is about focusing 100% of your energy into your mate. 'Date-Free' eliminates some major distractors to quality and leans the odds back in favour of listening and paying attention to one another.

As the expression goes, there are so many birds being killed with one stone here; rushes of flame-igniting chemicals being released because of the novel nature of the exercise, side-lining an often-arguable topic such as finances and quality time with the one you love. Gotta love efficiency.

Go: Creativity is King

The parameters for 'Date-Free' are not rocket science. Sit down as a couple and plan your date with creativity and flair. There is a minimum duration of three hours for the activity, so keep that in mind in the planning phase. No money may exchange hands to enact this date.

Some often-unforeseen money grabbers are filling the car with gas/petrol, hiking boots for a day of mountain climbing, or even inserting coins into a parking meter. Being stringent with this is to allow your minds and hearts to move to new places.

What are some examples of dates that cost no money?

Picnic at the park made from foods currently in the fridge. Grab a blanket, the basket full of goodies and a book you can read together.

Driving to a secluded beach cliffside and hitting golf balls into the sea.

Head out to the local SPCA and come up with a joint animal to adopt (virtually do this unless you can adopt an animal without exchanging any money for it) and discuss why you chose it. Then, go to all the places you would if you had adopted the animal and pretend you are caring for that little creature.

Get dressed up, head to a posh car dealership, and create a scenario for the selling agent that convinces them you want to buy their most expensive vehicle. Go on a test drive and really own the experience.

The ideas I proposed were to get your creative juices flowing and to begin the process of thinking outside the box. I advise you not to choose any of the examples above; instead, use them to inspire your own ideas, as that will be far more fruitful.

One last important note in doing this activity is to go on your 'Date-Free' within two weeks of planning it. If you get creative and design it and then wait weeks and weeks to enjoy it, its relevance will be missed. There is a window that presents itself for transformation and growth and when we let life dictate our schedule, more than nought, it'll never happen! Be the change by acting on your planned date and having a ball.

Going the Distance: Commit to Being Fresh and Vital

The essence of this exercise is creativity and novelty within your relationship. But, if you think that playing 'Date-Free' once and then never visiting it again will be forever fruitful, it doesn't work that way. Making a commitment to your relationship's freshness and vitality is everything. Once that agreement is made, spontaneity becomes your modus operandi, and fun and excitement are your ways of being.

Stepping outside the daily grind and doing things differently will serve you through the years. If you want to be a SuperCouple, it requires concerted effort every day. Most people want benefits for no exchange, but I usually term that as fantasy. Engaging regularly in activities, games and unique dates forms new neural pathways within the brain and the actions that match that will follow.

This is how an average couple transforms into being revered for their spark and freshness. Will you be that couple, or will you be the ones observing another and wishing to have some of what they've got? The choice lies in your hands. It's up to you whether you go on a first 'Date-Free' night and then follow it up with other spontaneous and exciting activities, but if you do, the exercise is much more profound.

Eban
Adinkra Africa

Eban translates to mean 'fence', though in the case of this symbol, it represents more the safety and security provided by the home. The home is where the family is, and therefore the symbol also represents love and the security provided by the family.

Meet the Players:

Christine and Jay

USA

American couple Christine & Jay are navigating a 'Fly-In-Fly-Out' doctor schedule and a mom-life devoted to raising their two sons, one of which is autistic.

Meeting in a New York City hospital more than two decades ago, these two jet setters are now calling Australia home. They have fought hard to create the relationship they now parent from. Choosing a life where Jay works a plane ride away as an ER Doc while Christine runs the ship at home means that 'date night' is a rare commodity. The 'Date-Free' game was ideal for them, and they embraced it like seasoned veterans.

Christine saw one problem on the horizon. "Planning for this is tough with Jay as he doesn't typically like to plan," she said. So, simplicity reigned. "It was pretty basic and not that involved. I mean, I probably told him what you wanted, read it to him and then we just set aside the date."

"That simplicity rose into a 'love-in' just like that of John Lennon and Yoko Ono," laughed Jay.

"And when was the last time we were able to do that? Like never. Certainly not since we've had kids. And we never would have an entire day to do that, so that's what we did."

Christine observed that "Because we had the time and space, it was just nice to be held close to each other," whereas normally, their divergent schedules would mean she would push away hugs and being touched because she needed some space to recover from being the full-time parent.

Jay also noticed, "In this day and age where we are all so connected, that you can prioritise tech connections over the person sitting right next to you. So, it was nice to prioritise each other."

And once again, the game wins out. Providing new opportunities for space and time so that each partner can see the other in a new and refreshing light. I love how simplicity brought about such depth and love!

Game 7

Vision Boarding Your Common Dreams

On Your Marks: Map out Your Future

As a couple, we can do a myriad of fun activities together. We can go on vacation, watch a movie, go to the park with the kids, have dinner with friends, and so much more. And then there are out-of-the-ordinary exciting activities that are not only fun and exhilarating, but also map out your future as a couple.

Case in point: Creating a couple's vision board!

This project has a variety of phases which aim to bring you closer together and provide some quality time. Bringing to life what's in those heads of yours is colourful and enjoyable. It's one thing to have it lodged in your neurology but quite another when you see it clearly in front of you every day.

What does visualising it every day bring to those dreams? Focus, clarity and intention. Clarity comes in the form of seeing the vision board and thinking about it in a more refined and specific manner. Intention is like the rudder of a boat; it steers direction and keeps the vessel travelling on the right path. Having your dreams spearheaded through this visual becomes a focal point in your home. As a dream clarifies itself and the coordinates for its realisation are plugged in, this heat-seeking missile has no choice but to hit its mark.

As you both view your vision board daily in your home, so will those people visiting you. Whether it's your immediate family or friends and colleagues, having your dreams on display keeps you accountable to them.

Once you put your dreams out there, the cooperative components (mostly people) organise themselves and begin knocking on your door. If you hide what you are dreaming of and closet yourself with your deepest desires, you miss out on the help and support and idea sharing that others can provide. This is one of the biggest mistakes people make - not sharing their passions and dreams with those loving and supportive hearts surrounding them.

Get Set: Heart not Head

Vision boarding has some common pitfalls that many first-timers can fall into. Sorting for visuals depicting wads of money, expensive cars, and diamond rings may leave you remiss as you are merely tapping into common cultural views of the dream life. There's nothing inherently wrong with these items, but accessing your primordial, non-social element that is genetically unique to you, is where you'll discover your innate preferences. Using inner body reactions (basically everything but your head) to select your images is how you unleash your human imagination.

Popular American Life Coach Martha Beck furthers this by stating, "The board itself doesn't impact reality; what changes your life is the process of creating the images—combinations of objects and events that will stick in your subconscious mind and steer your choices toward making the vision real."

Making the vision very real was the star of the movie The Secret, John Assaraf. His six-year-old son opened a box of old vision boards when moving into their new home. "There, on my vision board, was a picture I'd clipped from an old copy of Dream Homes magazine five years earlier in Indiana. It was a unique house with 188 windows, 320 orange trees, two lemon trees and a slew of other unique features. There was no mistaking it. It was a picture of the house the two of us were sitting in at that very moment. Not like it. It was this house."

Physicist Werner Heisenberg explains this with his synopsis that "consciousness can shape reality". This simple reasoning may omit the crucial element of elbow grease. What place does "action" play in all of this? Martha Beck sums it up beautifully: "Regularly picturing delights that don't yet exist, emotionally detaching from them, and jumping into action when it's time to help the miracles occur." There it is. No more, no less!

Go: Images, Scissors, Glue and a Board

There are many ways to bring your dreams into view and with the introduction of more creative technologies, this process has become even more pinpoint in its accuracy.

Option 1 (the old-school method):

You'll need: images that can be found in magazines, newspapers, advertising pieces or photos. A poster board, magnetic board or sticky photo album, scissors, tape and/or glue. Optional are markers and coloured pens to round out your creation.

Collecting magazines and visually pleasing articles or advertising materials one month in advance will put you in good stead and allow time for variety. Having a spectrum of images, from travel, to food, to clothes, to houses, to quotes, will serve you well as you build your masterpiece.

Option 2 (involves a computer and/or printer):

Search for the images that suit your preferences and either paste them to a word document or print them off.

Use Canva www.canva.com (there is a free version) to choose images and even design your board using their templates.

Choosing your board can make all the difference. The point of this exercise is that you see your Vision Board every day. Magnetic boards can be affixed to a kitchen fridge, which has appeal in terms of daily sighting, whereas finding a poster board is easiest and can be affixed to any wall. Whichever board you choose, ensure it can be viewed daily.

A caveat here is that viewing is not the same thing as straining for its realisation. Many a vision board creator gets off course by forcing the result rather than allowing it to show up. The visual should be an easy focal point that inspires good feelings within. If you sense disappointment that something hasn't shown up or strain creeping in, put it in the closet and allow the next reminder to be the actual manifestation showing up.

Block out at least two hours for creating your vision board, as the fun tends to lead to cutting and pasting the hours away. Some suggestions are to go through all magazines, cut out what each of you likes, and then go through each so there's no double-up. Coming together is essential as this is a Couple Vision Board and represents your shared dreams and aspirations.

Once there is consensus, glue away and let your artistic flair come through. Don't forget to post up your masterpiece straight away as you don't want to lose any time admiring and gazing at what will soon be your reality.

Going the Distance: Constant Renewal

Getting the juice from your Couple Vision Board lies in viewing it daily but also amending and adapting it every three months. Now that you are loving the daily visualisation, you will begin noticing images everywhere that you want to include and update. Evolution is about adapting and adding/upgrading your board.

There may come a time when your vision board feels outdated (because you are now actually looking at your newly renovated kitchen in real-time, and that child you wanted is screaming in their crib) and so make another date in your calendar and get back to the drawing board. They say that our values (what's important to us) shift and transmute every 6-12 months, and so this clearly lets us know that our Couple Vision Boards need a facelift on a yearly basis. You will notice that you will engage the process with more enthusiasm the second time around as you are an experienced masterpiece creator and lavish the final product that adorns the walls of your home.

This process of upgrading/updating your values as a couple is a sign of a sound and healthy relationship. Testimonials of enduring couples reflect that redefining themselves as individuals and as a partnership happens multiple times within a lifetime. The science backs this up with the proven birthing cycle occurring within relationships every three years. Your Couple Vision Board is your tangible representation of the software upgrade that not only your computer requires but your partnership as well.

Like every exercise, activity and game in this book, their value increases exponentially depending on how consistently you engage. Creating your vision boards is no different. Get stuck into your firm masterpiece and its continued evolution and growth will lead into itself. Momentum will build effortlessly when you feedback on how inspiring your visioning has been in the past. Your next board will manifest itself.

Meet the Players:

Aleisha and Hayden

New Zealand

Kiwi couple Aleisha & Hayden take on this visual goal-setting challenge and add their own flair.

Creating a Couple Vision Board has elements of communication and togetherness that surpasses doing your own representation. I chose an experienced manifestation duo for this one. During this interview, they openly share the newer process they have been doing for the past nine years, which they now include their kids in.

(Please head to the podcast "In the Game" for the full audio interview with this dynamic couple: www.buzzsprout.com/238055)

Hayden shared they leant on their five years goals to get into this vision boarding and Aleisha shared that, "We wrote ourselves a letter in 2019 for what we wanted to create by 2024. We kind of read through that together and reflected on where things were at. And then we co-created what we want to see for 2023. We searched the Internet to find the right images and now we can print our board out and put it on our fridge."

And speaking of putting it on your fridge, I was curious about how a man's man like Hayden would explain his vision board to his mates if they came over for a beer. He plainly stated, "I'll just explain what each photo means to me." And if they look at him like they want a great life too, he'll tell them, "You guys need a vision board too, then." Simple as that.

But it was this story from Aleisha that really tells the tale of the power of visioning your dreams. "Recently, we've been able to help a family member out financially to move out of an area that wasn't great for them into a new home where there's a big piece of land. We decided to subdivide it and develop the back.

"So, we had a goal around family first and foremost for us. We also had a goal around a potential land bank development opportunity. We'd never imagined that those two things could come together and so quickly too. We're now in the process of plans to develop that land by the end of next year.

Hence, the family member will have this beautiful new beachside home, which is all the same project. It's been amazing. It's kind of blowing my mind.

When we wrote these goals out a few years ago, we were thinking, 'Oh, maybe in the ten years we'd love to do another build, maybe we could look to subdivide' and yet, we had no idea how it would come together."

This incredible true account reminds us to be creative with minimal control because the majesty of life tends to show up even more beautifully than we could ever plot or plan.

Game 8

Vows Brought to Life

On Your Marks: More than Words?

Making solemn vows and promises to the person you want to spend the rest of your life with is a tradition that has been in practiced for centuries. A typical religious vow contains the famous words 'to have and to hold from this day forward, for better for worse, for richer, for poorer, in sickness and in health, to love and to cherish, till death us do part'. Promises such as these have been part of relationship fabric since they were translated into English in 1549 for The Book of Common Prayer. One of the drawbacks of ancient tradition can be our disconnection from its original meaning and intent.

Bringing conscious awareness to the powerful words spoken on that special day when you may have betrothed yourself to another can be one of the most refreshing experiences of your life. By reflecting on what was once said in front of friends and family, or perhaps you and your partner spoke solely before a witness, here is an opportunity to re-commit yourself in a powerful and positive way.

How can we really make forever promises when minds struggle to plan more than two weeks ahead? One of the most empowering things we did in my relationship before getting married, was to coin the phrase 'everyday-forever 'as it allowed us to create a daily intention that we could manage. This made it much easier for us to be responsible to the vows and promises we were making to one another on our wedding day.

The most important question to ask yourself in this game of Vows Brought to Life is: "How can what we said on our wedding day be relevant to our relationship today?"

Get Set: Where your Word Can Be Law

With the wisdom of experience, it's time to delve deeper into those vows you spoke so knowingly on your wedding day. Unpack some of the meaning of the words you professed however many years ago and what they mean to you now. This game allows you to compare how you were thinking then with how you process things now.

Marriage and its traditions are so intricately woven into the fabric of our culture that it isn't uncommon for the bride and groom to repeat reverent words before their God without even considering their meaning. As a great minister friend of mine from Vancouver, BC, said, "Traditions can become the distractor from the things that are 'really' present." Popular American relationship expert Iyanla Vanzant furthered that by exclaiming, "In the process of planning and having a wedding, I forgot there would actually be a marriage, a union of minds, bodies, souls and issues that would come together as soon as the ceremony was over."

To give you some foundational elements for this game of 'Vows Brought to Life', some mainstream definitions of a vow can lead the way:

An earnest promise to perform a specified act or behave in a certain manner.

An oath - pledge - promise – a sacrament.

A promise is defined as:

A declaration assuring that one will or will not do something.

At the centre of both definitions are action words such as perform, behave and do.

When re-visiting your own vows and how they have played out over the years, you have a real opportunity to have an integrity conversation. Integrity is 'being your word' and knowing that you can clean things up when you are <u>not</u> your word. Being able to clean up mistakes is the missing piece of the puzzle which leads to lots of over-promising and even more under-delivery. When you take your word seriously while also maintaining the grace of understanding that you will never get it perfect, a world of integrity and authenticity opens to you within all your relationships.

Go: We've Come so Far

Before beginning steps one-to-three in this process, recall, find or research what your vows were. Be as exact as you can with the words you professed when you first said them. For those who spoke traditional vows, visit http://weddingvowexamples.com.au/wedding-vow-examples for a list of Catholic, Baptist, Buddhist and other vows that may have been your vow of choice on the day.

If you can't remember your vows, find the memento book you wrote them in, drag out the wedding video and watch it again, ask your wedding party, or if you're still unsure, meditate on it and see if you can't pull up those magic words you spoke. This initial phase can be very telling - if you can't remember what you said, how the heck are you actioning them in your relationship? Fret not, most people can't find their vows, can't recall their vows and definitely aren't living their vows.

If you have your vows sitting in front of you in written form, it's time for you to bring them to life in this three-step process:

Step 1: Circle all the keywords (things that pop out as relevant) in your own vows and then go deeper into what those words mean to you. Has this changed since you said them initially? Either way, it's most exciting to build on the meanings you create as of today.

Step 2: With your mate, verbally go through the years together since you've professed these words starting at your honeymoon and then building back to today. Remember the better, worse, richer, poorer, sickness and health moments if you employed more traditional vows and have a good laugh and appreciation for how far you've come. This step has an element of momentum to it. Once you feel the energy of how you've overcome so much and that nothing did you in, there is a great sense of anticipation for the next great experience coming your way as a couple.

Move to the next section for step three.

Going the Distance: Journeying

Step 3: The final step is how you use your vows to carry you powerfully into your future. Now that you have unpacked your vows and detected meaning, had a laugh and appreciated how far you've come, it's time to have these promises serve you moving forward. Using the preceding steps, make some solemn vows into your future: One-year, five-year and 10-year markers are ideal. Allow what you said all those years ago to inspire the next leg of your relationship journey.

Borrowing wisdom from Kahuna Kaniela Akaka Jr and the ancient Hawaiian tradition: "The aloha that calls us to stand face to face with the sacredness of life. Not life as you know or have known, but life that is yet to be lived out." This is the journey. Hawaiian ancestors travelled thousands of miles across unchartered seas, on double-hulled canoes to discover the Hawaiian Islands, not always knowing what they would encounter along their journey. Not knowing what lay ahead, their faith and commitments to the journey held them steadfast as they weathered storm and sunny waters.

Once you have clearly shared your commitments with your mate, as a bonus exercise brought to us by our Hawaiian brothers and sisters, look into your loved one's eyes, go nose-to-nose with them and breathe in deeply, allowing the breath of life (ha) to pass in the space between you both (alo). This very intimate moment will rally all the energies needed to sail this next leg of your couple's journey.

Meet the Players:

Emma and Pete

North Queensland, Australia

Australian couple Emma & Pete have two children and are from North Queensland.

This devoted couple uttered their vows more than 17 years ago in small town Mackay, Queensland. Surrounded by family and community, they made their solemn promise that has carried them into a new community in Brisbane these past years as their young children find their footing in the big smoke.

When considering playing this game, Pete and Emma looked high and low and couldn't find their original vows (which is quite common), and yet Emma recalls, "Our vows really said thank you for seeing all the strength in me, what is amazing about me and embracing and celebrating that. But they were also encouraging me to keep stretching, to keep challenging myself. And some of the words that really stood out to me were strength and comfort, bringing joy to each other's lives, taking time for each other and being there for one another.

And we also wanted our vows to be identical, rather than one person, you know, having a different role in the relationship - that idea of being a team and being equal was certainly something very important to us."

For Pete, he reflects that "Being married in your early 20s is easy. But as your mortgage gets larger, you start having kids and you're managing stressful jobs, things start to get hard!"

To reiterate that fact, he shares a vulnerable story about what he went through two years ago, "We decided to move our lives to Brisbane, and I had a job offer. I remember crawling up into a ball on the floor in tears and said to Em, 'I don't want to do this. I can't do this.' And Emma instantly had my back and said We CAN do this. We can do it together." Those are truly vows being brought to life.

I think Emma nailed it when she said, "It is really tricky constantly balancing all of the ambitions you had when you started your journey together," and so revisiting your vows five, ten, twenty years down the track can really be a rudder guiding your boat onward.

And yet, don't lose the mystery and wonder in it. Pete was clear, "What I want is to be surprised." Emma was profound, saying, "I think the reason why we try not to make too many detailed plans is we don't want to be limited by our ideas of what is possible. Because again and again, over the last 17 years, we've just found that anytime we've kind of had this plan, something even bigger has happened, something even better than what we could have even dreamed for our relationship and our family. And we're just so excited to see what that plan is and to have faith in it."

Game 9

Intimate-o-Meter

On Your Marks: Cracking Open the Mundane

When we first meet someone who captures our complete attention, there is nothing more interesting than 'them'. Everything about them is new and different. There is intrigue in unravelling new pieces of them with each new phrase they utter.

But what happens when the phrases aren't so new anymore and you've heard that joke they tell at parties one too many times? We are creative beings and crave birthing - new ideas, or pro-creating, humans have a deep desire to create. In the repetition of monogamous relationships, we can fall into the trap of mundane and boring. To combat this, most couples create drama to feel alive, but there are other more beneficial models for creating juicy intrigue.

The Intimate-o-Meter is a simple and fun way to delve below the surface for the gems waiting for your discovery. Compelling questions that require your partner to rise to a higher form of her or himself is rewarding for both members of the relationship. The process also cycles onto itself as one interesting answer stirs curiosity for the next question, and before you know it, you feel the cells of your body come alive with anticipation and intrigue. This is what stirs passion and romance. This is a reversal method of looking at lovemaking as intimacy (the deeper questions) triggered impulse and desire rather than waiting for passion to filter down to intimacy.

The Intimate-o-Meter is a no-fail system as the questions can only crack open new elements of your mate, which leads to interesting, intriguing and compelling dialogue. That same dialogue then spurs further curiosity that wants to be expressed physically through the body. This game is the full meal deal.

Get Set: Keeping Up with Who You've Become

In a relationship, there is always something new to uncover. Even though we are in the 21st century, before Socrates, Greek Philosopher Heraclitus knew that "Everything flows, nothing stands still" and that "Nothing endures but change".

Keeping up with that change is what many couples find their biggest challenge. Have you been keeping up with who you've become? Whether you're aware of it or not, things are constantly in flux within a relationship, shifting and changing in the stream of time. The Intimate-o-Meter is a simple way to stay abreast of the changing landscape through curiosity and a thirst for knowing more about the one you love.

A great friend of mine's mother was celebrating her 47th year of marriage when she recounted to me that her doctor had asked her that very day, "How have you been married to the <u>same</u> man for 47 years?" to which she promptly replied, "I haven't!" What she was getting at was that the man she had married all those years ago had changed repeatedly into new dimensions of himself. He just wasn't the same man he had been all those years ago. They had both re-defined themselves many times throughout their long marriage. This phenomenal couple built a life by each other's side by asking intimate questions of one another. It was clear that each one of them would change over a half-decade, but asking better questions of one another ensured they grew together rather than apart. Never shying away from the bigger questions, they now stand 47 years down the track, loving retirement, taking joy in their grandkids and generally inspiring all those they spend time with.

Go: The Intimate Interview

The crux of this game is to embody the 'interviewer'. Become the Oprah or the Michael Parkinson (Britain's King of Question) of your life. Though seemingly obvious, it's more than asking questions; it's wanting to understand what the responder means when they answer. With that in mind, this little game is about mixing it up and stepping out of the ordinary day-to-day drawl. Here are some sample questions to get you started:

What turns you on/off?

What is your favourite/least favourite word?

What sound or noise do you love/hate hearing?

What profession other than your own would you like to attempt?

What activity in the past month has kept you completely absorbed?

Tell me about your best friend when you were a kid

What scares you? Excites you?

Tell me about the last time you laughed so hard you teared up

What are you most proud of?

What would you like God to say when you arrive at the pearly gates?

Now that you have warmed up with the above questions and allowed the conversation to flow how it will, the next part of the exercise is to test your creative skills and come up with ten questions of your own.

Becoming a prominent interviewer in your relationship is the secret ingredient to spicing things up and evolving with the times. Knowing where your mate is emotionally during changing landscapes is down to the quality of your questions. I have heard the complaint from my couple clients that their mate doesn't share with them or talk to them. To that, I say, become a better 'asker of questions' and it will turn intimacy around.

Alternate turns by asking each other your ten questions making sure you have your listening skills tuned in and don't be afraid to ask your partner to clarify anything you don't understand. Be inquisitive and relish in seeing the world from your partner's vantage point during this amazing game.

Going the Distance: Take the Inquiry to Bed

Taking these interviewing skills into your everyday life is fantastic. Asking someone about themselves out of curiosity and a willingness to listen to what they have to say is a whole new frame of reference. Bringing that into your relationship will serve both of you. Intrigue for the partner asking the question and passion and excitement for the one answering about themselves on a deeper level.

One of my favourite questions is: "Tell me something about you that I don't yet know?" The reason this question is gold is because it never gets old. You can ask this every day of your life and the answer demands that it be different. I recommend this one as you snuggle into bed for the evening as something fresh and nice to fall asleep with - each other's intimate souls.

The following question is great for discovering your mate's driving force in life. It can also indicate where they are currently sitting on the emotional scale of their life. "What do you say to yourself to get you out of bed in the morning?" Innocuous as it might seem, the answer is very telling. Make sure they get to the exact self-talk they use to get their eyes open and those legs swinging out of bed when the other choice was to stay just where they were. If you get the answer 'I don't say anything to myself,' just probe a little more and see if an answer trickles out of them that they never even knew existed. As you can see, this may also benefit them - know thy self and be free. Using this simple question, the answer can translate into what motivates someone to do anything. That's a big answer that's worth waking up for.

Odo Nyera Fie Kwan
Adinkra Africa

The Odo Nyera Fie Kwan symbol represents the proverb, 'those led by love will never lose their way,' sometimes written as 'love never loses its way home'. This symbol is usually engraved on wedding bands and other events related to the union of two people. The Akan people consider it a powerful mantra to represent a union.

Meet the Players:

This long-term entrepreneurial couple recently moved from Melbourne with their two children.

(This couple wished to remain anonymous, so I shall refer to them as hubby and wife for the purposes of describing their experience.)

How do long-term couples tackle this game with curiosity? I was fascinated to see whether it was only me who loved being an interviewer or whether other couples would get into it too.

And they did.

Hubby had a clear stance on what mattered when he played this game. "If you can't sit still and actively listen with non-judgment, then you know, there's no relationship there," he said. He was inspired by my metaphor about how you 'never step into the same bit of river twice' (as written in this chapter) and paralleled it to, 'the banks of the river may never meet, but it's what intermediates between them that defines the relationship.' So, you can be separate, but it's the intermediary of communication that binds the relationship together.

Wifey was expectant around the whole experience of the game as she acknowledged, "Time has gone on and we have evolved - we're different humans now. It's powerful to touch back in and to explore who we are now at this stage of our relationship."

Even though they both tackled the game in their individual ways - he used the questions offered as icebreakers to provide clear space to dive deeper into subjects that have been on his mind, whereas she was able to gain real insights into the way he sees the world vs the way she does. Commenting, "It's not for me to judge, and the space this game afforded us allowed me to let go of any kind of built-up resentments that might have been stirring and bring more acceptance and understanding instead. It felt really liberating."

This game allowed Wifey to reflect, "We actually do need to schedule in more time together just on our own." At the same time, Hubby saw the benefits for his own personality by noting, "That's the problem with being in your head - you can make assumptions about the motivations of other people and what they're feeling. It was good to speak about things and hear it in black and white."

And it's a WIN for Intimate-O-Meter!

Game 10

Listen Up

On Your Marks: Hearing Beyond an Age of Distraction

Being a good listener is commonly hailed as the holy grail of communication these days: whether at work or in relationships. Most of our mothers have been yelling this command since we reached the 'terrible twos', and so we know it's essential, but can we honestly say we know any more about it than decades ago?

In an age of iPhone apps, Skype, 24-hour news, iTunes and podcasts, there isn't much room for us to hear those people who are most important in our lives. It's not from lack of effort, as more than ever we desire to be better listeners but 'trying' might be the block to hearing what someone is saying.

Hearing what your mate is saying beyond your filtered perception of them is true relationship. Most of us only know our partners through our own filtered story of them. This doesn't allow for much movement or growth within the relationship and is probably not what you intended when you began your courtship.

You only have to notice your self-talk for 15 minutes to understand that you surely wouldn't be able to hear everything someone says beyond this incessant chatter. Most people have this 'monkey mind' darting all about unless, of course, you've committed to an extensive meditation practice for more than two years.

Imagine how much time and energy you would save if you could hear your mate on the first go. No wasted time satisfying what you think they want but being able to deliver what they clearly desire. No more trial and error, just desires being met over and over again. There is nothing more empowering inside a relationship than this.

Get Set: To Hear is Not to Listen

Having a great capacity for listening is the secret weapon of communication. Science has shown the power of our vision filters, but our hearing filters 100,000 bits per second as well. The path of sound vibration is electromagnetic and converts into sound vibration once it hits the ear apparatus. Nerve cells convert that energy to be processed by the brain, and then the conscious mind filters at less than 100 bits per second. Our filters are the limiting factor here, so it becomes a case of opening the conscious to expose ourselves more intimately to the massive amount of sound vibrations encircling us.

The National Institute of Deafness has been a leader in the study of sound and hearing. "Much sensory information exists beyond our ability to experience it. Our level of awareness is influenced by our individual abilities, our genes, our environment, and our previous experiences, as well as the interactions among them." There are two ways to interpret this information; confining and limited to our inherent capacities OR expansive and massive room for improvement. I choose the latter as it provides an opening to become a more proficient communicator and hence nurture a successful and growing relationship.

I think it's important to make a distinction between hearing and listening. Hearing is our capacity to perceive sound waves, whereas listening is our attention to what we are hearing. There is a finite volume of sound vibration incoming, but our attention is something that can be trained.

I know this intimately, having been a professional athlete for 14 years. Improvement on the world stage was mostly about which team could hold their concentration and attention for the longest. Games are won and lost during moments of attention or lack thereof. Having intimately experienced this area of concentration increase through intense training, I look forward to sharing this game from the pro's playbook.

Go: Turn Your Hearing Aid Up

The objective of this game is to listen 'completely' to what is being said during the entire exercise. This may sound simple but let me introduce the specific instructions and see if you still feel the same after you have both completed each round. This game is anything but simple.

Instructions:

Set an alarm clock for three minutes and begin.

In a standing position, look your partner in the eye and tell them four things that inspire and four things that scare you. This is your moment to have three minutes of undivided attention from your mate - make the most of it as this is golden time.

You must remain talking for a complete three minutes while maintaining eye contact.

The listener must not reply or fill empty spaces with words or actions.

Once the three mins are up, your partner, who was listening, now has two minutes to repeat back, word for word what they heard their partner saying.

It is vital that the non-repeating partner does not save their mate in their silence and allow the complete two minutes to transpire - it is part of the strength of the exercise to sit in the silence of their not being up to speed with their listening.

Partners now change roles and start again.

Once both partners have completed the exercise, answer the following questions while bearing in mind this is not about being a good or bad listener but merely a launching place to begin training this skill.

Each partner answers the following separately:

What was getting in the way of repeating word for word what your partner was saying?

What were the dominant thoughts or self-talk being repeated within your own mind?

What was the impact of you 'not completely listening' on your mate? Write down what you detected through their body language and then ask them what it felt like not to be listened to completely

Now, share with one another the experience of listening and being heard. They are both powerful places to stand inside the conversation of communication.

Going the Distance: Expanding Your Awareness

Were you challenged during this game? Did you have so much internal chatter that when it came time to repeat back, you drew a blank? Even if you found it quite natural to repeat back what you heard, there is always more to this skill of listening, as there are tonality nuances as well as body language and even energetic shifts all going on simultaneously. Words are only 7% of communication, so this repeating back process is the tip of the iceberg.

Are you starting to understand why I've classified the art of listening as the secret weapon within communication? This untapped potential is so exciting, and one way to take in more of the conversation, including words, body language and energy, is to go into 'expanded awareness'. Most of us have learned how to focus on things through schooling and work demands, but opening our awareness is not a practiced skill.

One way to tap into this is to look straight ahead at one specific spot above eye level and concentrate on it for 30-60 seconds. Then, leaving your eyes hooked to that spot, wiggle your fingers to the side of your body and bring your attention to them even though your eyes are still gazing forward. Expanding your awareness to the periphery is what allows you to pick up on subtle cues as well as relax enough to hear beyond the self-talk. It's a tool for becoming present and allowing the words in while also trusting that you will be able to recall when appropriate.

Listening is not so much about what you hear but rather your trusting of recall. The information is all there inside of you, but the stress of remembering or not trusting yourself leads to a blank look when communicating. Practice expanded awareness in mundane tasks and watch it flourish in your listening to others. A whole new experience of your relationship will open to you.

Meet the Players:

Hailing from a teeny tiny town in Eastern Canada, this couple have used therapy to develop their more than 21 years together.

(They wish to remain anonymous, so we will respect their wishes by calling them 'Hubby' and 'Wifey' for the duration of this conversation)

This game is one of the hardest. As I explain in my interview intro, "You soon become aware that it's virtually impossible to hear what your partner is really saying over the noise of your own chatter." And hubby stated it straight out when he remembered, "But repeat three minutes of what she was saying - that was a lot. I was just overwhelmed."

And not that I meant to set them up, but I did!

That is the point of this one. To be able to get a couple that has been together for over two decades to admit that they could improve their listening of one another. It's no easy feat, but worth the outcome of that admission.

Wifey said it in plain English, "We're talkers, but we're probably not listeners - or deep enough listeners. What we hear isn't necessarily what the other one is saying."

She even went on to admit, "I talk all the time. So obviously, I need to tone down all these words and make sure what I'm saying is my true intention and that my husband understands what the message is."

And I just love the honesty of wifey in how her 'stuff' was brought to the surface with the task of this game. "So, my brain goes into control mode, 'You're not doing it right (she's thinking about him). You know this isn't how the game is supposed to be played.'"

This classic mind chatter is what prevents you from fulfilling the task to repeat exactly what your partner is saying.

It's Wifey's willingness to take the exercise on that was so refreshing, "This just showed me for sure that I'm a distracted listener. I was worried about things that didn't matter, and I should have been more concerned with listening to his words and what he wanted to express to me."

And then my favourite moment is when Hubby becomes inspired by his wife's admissions, "I see her being introspective and that says to me 'If she can do it, so can I.' When you see your partner who's so strong-willed be able to put a pause on that and start to reflect, it inspires me to continue to work on my own stuff."

Game 11

Couple ZZZs

On Your Marks: Really Sleeping Together

If you grow up in a strict Christian home, one of the biggest no-no's for unmarried couples is sleeping together. Ironically, this little activity invites all relationships to defy that tenant on the surface yet honour it fully in practice. Being able to sleep with and next to your mate is what this game is all about. This may single-handedly be one of the greatest gifts you can give your mate - the magic of a peaceful night's rest!

Every one of us experiences the overactive mind or the stresses of life getting the better of our sleep cycle. Often, your mate lying next to you is as awake as you are. Did you know that your alert energy can rouse a previously sleepy mate? Lying in proximity to another does have an energetic impact, and so it's no accident that when one of you is restless, the other can be found tossing and turning just as much.

The value of having a tool that allows couples to combine for much desired and needed ZZZs is twofold: bringing peace in the moment and comfort for any future anxiety over restlessness and inability to fall asleep. Knowing that you and your mate can come together and provide an automatic hypnotic sleep pattern is such a blessing. Being well-rested positively impacts on how you interact with your environment. The opposite is proven by couples with newborn babies who are sleep deprived. Lack of sleep is like a cloud hanging over the world that these two new parents' zombie through. Not to mention the massive strain this holds on the relationship's health. Offering a tool that guarantees a couple sleeps well is like providing a healthy pill that keeps on giving.

Get Set: Brainwave Entrainment

Sleep is a commodity keenly sought by those who lead big lives. The problem is that the more you want it, the more it alludes you. It's one of those perilous endeavours you hope is functioning well because if you go head-to-head with it, you're thinking, and busy mind will win every time.

Introduce a small breathing chant routine that combines with your mate for even more effectiveness, and you discover the sleepy crack of least resistance. There is a particular brainwave frequency that matches the state of sleep, as proven by Banzai Labs and their 'Advanced Binaural Programs' promoting sleep. As a means of brainwave entrainment, this routine synchronises with the sleep frequency, and before you can figure out what is happening, you are drawn into a deep sleep.

Combining your breath and vocal range with another, in this case, your loved one, is literally a unity of sound that lulls the brain to sleep. The two waves bouncing together are a masterful form of entrainment that leads to a stillness washing over your entire body, permitting it to sleep. It's amazing how fast and foolproof this little activity is. It's the SuperCouples greatest secret for explaining consistent dynamism and energy: a great night's sleep.

Yoga uses this principle of group breath and chanting as a way of building one-ness and unity. Ancient wisdom recognised the power of this practice, and now relationships can borrow the methodologies to come together as one. The body's organs have their own unique frequencies, and harmonising with them also promotes repair and regeneration. It's an all-round great routine that your body, mind and spirit will thank you for.

Go: Chanting Yourself to Sleep

The benefits of this little routine far outweigh its complexity. The simplicity will astound you though it does require a bit of courage to get over yourself and be willing to chant with your mate.

Lying flat on your back in bed, holding your partner's hand, breathe in deeply through your nose (filling your lungs to the max) and then chant 'ahhhhhhh' as a complete exhalation. Feel your stomach and lungs compress as you exhale all the air from your body. Be conscious of your mate's inhalation, as it may be longer or shorter than yours as a synchronisation process develops. Once the chant commences, let go entirely and surrender to the exhalation of the breath.

Repeat this sequence three to four times. To remain in harmony, stick with three repetitions unless one of you squeezes the other's hand in suggestion for a fourth or fifth sequence.

During this process, you will notice a harmonising of the 'ahhhhh' in such a way that you won't be able to detect where your voice begins and your partner's ends. It's a unique experience; just ride the wave of it while stillness overwhelms you and sleep becomes imminent.

Once complete, succumb to the nothingness and lie there in appreciation. Enjoy a definitive sleep that is assured of being more connected and deeper than you previously thought possible.

Going the Distance: Bedtime Secrets for Life

It's one thing to do this routine once, but there is such assurance in knowing you can jack this out whenever you want a solid night's rest. No more need to find that connecting feature with your mate; you've got a solid game plan that leads to one-ness. Bring it on!

The real fun begins when you engage in some chanting while spending Christmas vacation with your folks or a night in a close-knit bed and breakfast - there may be some ogling looks the next day! The joke is on them, though, as they stayed awake imagining what poses you were in while you and your partner were in 'la-la' land.

Wanting tools for sleep is only a concern when the ZZZs elude you; knowing that you have this chanting regime in your back pocket can be powerful in itself. Practicing it before you need it is where the gold lies. Once it is an ingrained habit, you may only opt for it once a month, but when you do, it's there and synchronised for your sleeping pleasure.

As this routine is suggested in a two-some, feel free to discover the enjoyment of a group chant. It need not be long, but a yoga class or meditation regime that brings the entire class into harmony through sound is something that resonates long after you leave the room. It's as if a tuning fork has been struck, and the vibration of it continues to ring in you well beyond the moment. As science catches up with these ancient traditions and begins to spit compelling data on the health benefits of these routines, you can rest assured knowing that you and your mate have been sleeping peacefully at one for years.

Osram ne Nsoromma
Adinkra Africa

Osram ne Nsoromma translates to 'the moon and the star'. It depicts a half moon as if it is a bowl that might catch the star above. The symbol represents faithfulness, fidelity, love and harmony.

Meet the Players:

Sarah and Sange

Gold Coast, Australia

Sarah & Sange recently wed and now live at the beach with their chubby-cheeked newborn.

There's nothing like playing a sleeping game with parents of a newborn – but I promise you that these mamas aren't the sleep-deprived story you'd expect when a child is under one year old.

Some sleep history on the girls before they came to this 'Couples ZZZs' activity will give it context.

Sange reports, "My sleep for the past four or five years before pregnancy was erratic. I would be in bed for around eight hours, but I would wake up two or three times during the night and struggle to fall back to sleep. It has been a challenge for me for a while. I've tried lots of different things, such as meditation, eating at different times of the day, making sure it was dark and cool and things like that. Funnily enough, when I met Sarah and we started sharing a bed, we both improved our sleep overnight."

On Sarah's side, "Before I met Sange, I was getting four and a half to five hours of sleep a night, but I wanted more. I also wanted to make the best of each day, so I was driven to get up early – and then I didn't want to miss out on anything, so wasn't heading to bed too early either. One thing subconsciously driving me was not wanting to go to bed unless I was tired because of that frustration of sleep alluding me."

By the time they met and had their daughter, they were sleeping much better, so how would this game impact them?

There were many reasons to delay this simple process, but in the end, this is how they went: "It took a few tries as we just kept squeezing each other's hands to communicate one more, one more. It took us that long to feel like we were in sync, I suppose. It started to flow, and a different vibration started. It was like a different sound was coming out than was typical."

You could sense that it was hard to describe in words, but they did come up with, "It felt really calm. We got to a rhythm – like our voices were harmonizing. Our timing just started to sink in and then we drifted off to sleep."

And who doesn't want to drift to sleep?? Sounds like a chant worth trying if it creates that kind of soothing rhythm!

Game 12

Get Jiggy with It

On Your Marks: Collaborating for a Common Outcome

Why are we more apt to play games and put puzzles together as kids than we are during adulthood? I'm assuming that many would say it's because we're too busy working at being mature adults to play frivolous games. Are we perhaps missing out on some of the wisdom our inner child knew very keenly when they came into the world?

Many of us have become disconnected from the innocent and fun-loving child we once knew so well. As mature as we may find ourselves, authentic growing up is when we align with that child who was untainted and full of zest for life.

Connecting with the play of our yesteryear is one of the most powerful elixirs for healing self-doubt and gaining competency. Don't feel singled out; most of the population has a breach in the seven phases of early childhood development when conditions were placed on love in some form that initiated compensatory behaviour. Hence the wedge gets placed on authentic play, and a life of toil to achieve is underway. No matter how wide the gap between our inner child and adult self is, a puzzle will connect the dots in a powerfully fun way.

Introduce your mate into the puzzle project, and now even more value has been added to the mix. Not only quieting and relaxing for both of your psyches, but it's also a stimulus that can have you complimenting each other, working together, getting in each other's way, yet generally collaborating for a common outcome.

How does that serve your everyday life?

From preparing dinner to getting the kids to soccer practice to attending a function as a couple to family Christmas at the in-laws, each of these endeavours is a puzzle requiring a masterful fit. You only need to walk into the kitchen of a family with more than two kids to see the puzzle that is their calendar schedule colourfully brightening up the fridge door. In the relaxed and quiet of puzzle construction, you may practice the very skills necessary to be a couple team in flow, one piece at a time.

Get Set: The Edges of a Relationship

Imagine if a puzzle was more than a simple game. Imagine if the edges of the puzzle were like the boundaries of a relationship, defining its exterior and providing an enclosure where something can be contained. What lies within the borders of the puzzle? The rest of the pieces make up the meat of the picture and are generally colourful and full of multiple images. Without a strong enclosure, it would be chaos. But once those boundaries are clearly in place and right-side-up, the framework has been set, and the innards have somewhere to be placed. What a lovely model for beautiful relationships!

Now, add the precision training of putting a masterpiece together and you've got a masterful exercise worth engaging in. From keen colour detection to connecting the dots of words and images that fit together, the precise work at play can be applied in many areas of life. As you are beginning to sense, there is a vast amount of concentration required in this exercise. If your mind wanders constantly, then it will become more obvious, and you can practice coming back to the task at hand and holding your attention for longer and longer periods. Dare I say we have a meditative component here too?

We must not forget the brain's love of organisation. When it first views the 1000 pieces lying in the box, it immediately seeks order. How each individual goes about this is unique. Constructing with your mate lets you see how their brains move towards order. Is that through process and mechanism (immediately fitting pieces together in small groupings) or taking in the big picture and putting systems together through that wide-angle view? Like a camera does, it either focuses in tight or goes to a wide lens and generally, people have a predisposition as to how they view and operate in the world.

There's nothing more fascinating than bearing witness to how your mate moves in the world, how they fit a puzzle together and how they work on that project with you!

Go: Piecing Together your Relationship

There isn't a lot of complexity to doing a puzzle with your mate, but some simple guidelines may spice it up so that it become a much more profound experience as a couple.

First comes the purchase. A seemingly easy piece of the puzzle (love the pun here), but there is so much variation these days. If you are not an experienced puzzler, then choose something with no more than 500 pieces. The key is finding that delicate balance between challenging and causing the brain to figure out something that is just past its comfort zone without taxing it to the point where it gives in. You'll know how you've chosen if you've avoided assembling a single piece for more than two weeks.

The latest in puzzle-dom is a great new phenomenon called WASGIJ - can you figure out why it's named that? No longer does the picture on the front of the box visualise what you are assembling, but it is only a mere clue in the WASGIJ world. What you are building is a mystery, and this adds extra delight on completion as you marvel at the humour and wit behind what you have put together.

Once you have decided what puzzle is right for you as a couple, choose a table or area where the masterpiece can live while being built. Where you do your puzzle generally relates to its enjoyment level. If you hide it in a dark room you never enter, you will probably keep avoiding this less-than-desirable place, and the puzzle will be ignored too. Put it on a coffee table where there is traffic, and it becomes a new alternative to watching TV and conversing as a family. You will soon discover that the puzzle itself centralises in your home and becomes a place of communion. I guarantee that dinner party guests will retire to the puzzle.

There are no more rules than this as to how to build your puzzle as a couple. Enjoy piecing together the fabric of a collaborative relationship.

Going the Distance: Bedtime Secrets for Life

Playing at puzzle creation gets under your skin. It's not only the cognitive relief of chaos being ordered but the natural harmonising that occurs when you fit pieces together with your mate.

It is easy to have a puzzle on the go week in and week out. It's not about doing it all the time but rather relaxing over it when dinner is on the stove, enjoying a cup of tea with a puzzle twist, or fitting pieces together post-dinner party with your friends.

You can be the instigator in your environment for puzzle doing. It's catchy, and your couple friends will take your lead. When the people in your life are also playing, it provides a hotbed for long-term change and transformation.

Going the distance with this game is about adding regular playful activities to your life. Whether it's puzzle creating, sandcastle building, climbing trees or brushing a doll's hair, connect with that inner child who wants attention. Listen to what they want a bit more, take the foot off the peddle of achievement or trying to be good at everything and lend an ear to what 'playful' activity the young one has in mind. You will notice the healing once you begin honouring this calling.

The latest on positive psychology reveals that happiness is not about a maniacal state but rather a more regulated, consistent way of being. So, what is one way to reach that consistent, more regulated state?

Make something!

Creative work secretes a neurotransmitter called dopamine, which allows us to feel absorbed and fulfilled without the often-assumed need for hysterical emotion. By creating through puzzles versus forcing elation day in and day out, a happy, balanced life ensues. After all, the purpose of life is joy, and the result is expansion. One piece at a time.

Meet the Players:

Binny and Randi

Brisbane, Australia

Binny and Randi are a Brisbane SuperCouple raising their two girls amidst a career in law and engineering.

I love puzzles! My Mom and I did them as a child, so as an adult, I surely had to come up with a game that involved piecing things together. There is so much symbolism in 'Get Jiggy with It' that I'm curious what this long-time couple discovered about each other.

Firstly, it was not in husband Randi's comfort zone, as Binny told me, "The girls and I puzzle together more than Randi and I, and so it was no surprise when we didn't talk strategy before we got going. He started doing the bottom of the puzzle at the border, and I started doing the top. We didn't decide what we were doing; we just worked away at the corners first. By sheer luck and happenstance, we ended up doing the top and bottom."

Is it luck, though? When a couple has been together for over a decade like these two, does happenstance really account for some of their ways of working together? I love the Mark Twain quote that says, "As we do one thing, is how we do everything." I always keep this in mind when hearing about how a couple plays these games.

When Binny wanted to strategize halfway through the game, Randi laughed and said, "She's always needing a method to do something – even when it comes to buttering her toast!" He commented that she was more of a typical engineer than him in her approach.

Whereas she noticed in him, "You're being really quiet, and he said, 'I'm concentrating on doing the puzzle.' He was in the zone of completing a task - which is very him!"

Everyone was puzzling just the way they do life! So apropos!

The real power in this game was reflected by Binny when she said, "Recognising the value in what your partner is doing and why they're doing it is one thing, but communicating that value is just as important. When you're a parent, you get so caught up in raising your kids and making sure they feel valued and appreciated that sometimes your partner takes a back seat. A partner needs just as much uplifting, reassurance and support. This game was one way for us to acknowledge the other person's contributions."

Cheers to that, Binny!

You've made it!

12 enriching relationship games are a commitment worth celebrating.

You started off strong in Game 1, realising that your "state" *IS* within your control. Moving along poetically, your New Couple Script can be quite the uplifting experience. I wonder who suffered more in Game 3s The Workout Swap?? All should have been forgiven with Hubby Hobby meets Wifey Whim – they had to consider *your* whims after all! One of my playful favorites is Creating Your Paper Paradise because you discover not only what dreams lie within you, but also what's stirring for your mate. And then, each room can become a symbolic touchpoint for your future. It's the Game with the 'most-est'

Game 6 seems so simple in its description of Date-Free, and yet that is its mastery, the simplicity itself garners the depth of relating-ship and connection we are often too busy to enjoy. *'Vision Boards' oh 'Vision Boards' how powerful they can be*; but add your togetherness to the mix and it takes on a whole new strength. Asking you to find your "vows" for Game 8 was a little confronting for most and yet, it wasn't about "what was", but rather "what is". Bringing vows to life years down the track of a relationship can remind us of the power that words play in impacting how we show up each and every day. Intimate-o-Meter is a personal preference Game for me because of my inquisitive spirit and work as an interviewer. Putting that curiosity in *your* hands so you can turn it toward the very person you technically know "everything" about, makes it that much more exciting.

Ok, ok, Game 10 was the hardest! Not that we are ranking them but... it was hard on purpose. I have never met a single couple who've nailed it. The bigger outcome is realising that Listen Up is a vital skill worth practicing and improving upon. The game was designed to wake you up to the fact that we listen with a quarter of our capacity! And then, Couple ZZZs lets you sleep. It literally "hummms" you vibrationally to the same tune of slumber. I mean, great follow-up from the toughest game, right? And lastly, a bit of light fun to Get Jiggy with It. Most couples can't recall when they last did a puzzle with their mate. So used to "children-only-zone", this is a great

I salute you in your devotion to growing and expanding your relationship. I wanted to congratulate you along with all my "test couples" (aka, great friends who say YES to me as a show of love and respect for our relating-ship) for showing up fully and Pressing Play on your relationship. In my work over these past 10 years, couples who not only stick together but inspire their community, tend to be those who inject effort into their partnership well beyond any crisis coming their way. You may just be that that couple who others look upon for guidance and inspiration of what's possible. Drink that in, way to remind yourself that PLAY is for adults too especially Forever Couples like you!

I would love to hear how the Games impacted your relationship and the fun little moments you experienced together so please send me a note.

Here's to many more years of light and love in your relationship

www.ingramcontent.com/pod-product-compliance
Lightning Source LLC
Chambersburg PA
CBHW060522010526
44107CB00060B/2652